AMERICA IN WORDS AND SONG

The Pledge of Allegiance

The Story Behind Our Patriotic Promise

CHELSEA CLUB HOUSE

An Imprint of Chelsea House Publishers

A Haights Cross Communications Company

Philadelphia

Liz Sonneborn

Chelsea Clubhouse books are published by Chelsea House
Publishers, a subsidiary of Haights Cross Communications Company.

A Haights Cross Communications Company

The Chelsea House World Wide Web address is
www.chelseahouse.com

Printed and bound in the United States of America.

9 8 7 6 5 4 3 2

Library of Congress Cataloging-in-Publication Data
Sonneborn, Liz.
  The pledge of allegiance : the story behind our patriotic promise /
by Liz Sonneborn.
    p. cm. — (America in words and song)
Summary: Describes how and why Francis Bellamy came to write
the Pledge of Allegiance, explaining the meaning of the pledge
and the controversies surrounding it.
Includes bibliographical references and index.
  ISBN 0-7910-7336-X
1. Bellamy, Francis. Pledge of Allegiance to the Flag—Juvenile
literature. 2. Flags—United States—Juvenile literature.
[1. Pledge of Allegiance. 2. Bellamy, Francis. 3. Flags—United States.]
I. Title. II. Series.
  JC346.S66 2003
  323.6'5'0973—dc21   2003004044

Selected Sources

The Pledge of Allegiance: A Centennial History, 1892–1992,
    by Dr. John Baer. Web site:
    www.vineyard.net/vineyard/history/pdgech0.htm

Bellamy, Francis. *Twenty-Three Words: The Life Story of the
    Author of the Pledge of Allegiance as Told in His Own Words*.
    Edited by Margarette S. Miller. Portsmouth, VA: Printcraft
    Press, 1976.

"A Matter of Conscience: American Treasures of the Library
    of Congress." Library of Congress Web site:
    www.loc.gov/exhibits/treasures/trr006.html

The New York Times, June 26, 2002

Editorial Credits

Colleen Sexton, editor; Takeshi Takahashi, designer;
Mary Englar, photo researcher; Jennifer Krassy Peiler, layout

Content reviewer:

Dr. John Baer, author of *The Pledge of Allegiance:
A Centennial History, 1892–1992*

Photo Credits

©Steve Chenn/CORBIS: cover; ©Joseph Sohm/CORBIS: title
page, 12 (right), 22, 25 (right); AP/Wide World: 4, 5, 9, 15, 17,
18, 24, 30; ©Bettmann/CORBIS: 6, 7, 12 (left), 14, 16;
©CORBIS: 8; North Wind Picture Archives: 10; Department of
Rare Books and Special Collections, University of Rochester
Libraries: 11 (both); ©Underwood & Underwood/CORBIS: 13;
©Reuters NewMedia Inc./CORBIS: 19, 26; ©Hulton
Archive/Getty Images: 20; ©CORBIS, 21 (right), 23, 27;
©Flip Schulke/CORBIS: 21 (left); ©Ed Bock/CORBIS: 25 (left)

Table of Contents

Introduction

In June 2002, the Ninth Circuit Court of Appeals in San Francisco, California, made a surprising ruling. It declared that the Pledge of Allegiance could no longer be said in public schools in nine western states. The ruling came from a **lawsuit** brought by Michael Newdow against his local school district in Elk Grove, California. In his daughter's second-grade class, the teacher led the students in saying the pledge every day:

> I pledge allegiance to the Flag of the United States of America, and to the Republic for which it stands, one Nation under God, indivisible, with liberty and justice for all.

The words "under God" upset Newdow. He believed the phrase should not be used in public schools. In his view, this went against the basic ideals stated in the U.S. **Constitution** and its First Amendment. This document says that religion and the government should be kept separate. Because the government runs public schools, the court agreed with Newdow.

Michael Newdow objected to the words "under God" in the Pledge of Allegiance. Saying that these words should not be recited in public schools, he brought a lawsuit against a California school district.

The reaction to the ruling was fast and furious. President George W. Bush called it "ridiculous." Speaker of the House Dennis Hastert said the court "has gotten this one wrong." Senator Tom Daschle claimed it was "just nuts." Many leaders believed the U.S. Supreme Court, the highest court in the land, should review the ruling. People throughout America were also outraged. Many had spent their childhoods saying the pledge in school. Barring it from the classroom struck them as **un-American**.

These strong feelings showed just how much the Pledge of Allegiance means to many Americans. For more than 100 years, its words have helped the American people voice their love of their flag and their country.

Students in Elk Grove, California, say the Pledge of Allegiance. A court ruled in 2002 that students in California and eight other western states could no longer say the pledge in public schools.

The Idea

Sitting in his office in Boston, Massachusetts, James Bailey Upham suddenly had an idea. The year was 1888. Americans were still carrying painful memories of the Civil War (1861–1865), a long struggle between the Northern states and the Southern states. Now Americans were united as one nation again. Upham wanted people to regain a feeling of love for their country. He wanted them to show their **patriotism**. Upham thought about starting with schoolchildren. His idea was that every public school in America should raise the flag each morning.

Upham was a strong supporter of public schools. He thought the free educational system was one of America's biggest accomplishments. In classrooms, teachers taught children from many backgrounds about U.S. history and how the government works. Upham believed this common education brought Americans together and helped make the country great. He thought seeing a flag flying above their schools every day would remind students what they had learned. Upham hoped the flag would inspire them to love their country.

Taken in 1891, this photograph shows students in front of their one-room schoolhouse in Kansas. James Upham believed every schoolhouse, no matter how small, should fly an American flag.

The Youth's Companion

The Youth's Companion was once one of America's best-loved magazines. Founded in 1827, it was published for 102 years. By the late 1800s, the *Companion* printed and sent out nearly 500,000 copies of each weekly issue. Much of its success was due to the wide range of articles it offered readers. Designed to be a magazine that family members could read together, it included articles about current events, short stories, puzzles, and special pages just for children. It often featured pieces by famous American writers. Mark Twain, Emily Dickinson, and Jack London all published work in *The Youth's Companion*. The magazine's motto was "Nothing But the Best."

Upham worked for *The Youth's Companion*, a popular family magazine. His uncle, Daniel Ford, owned and edited the *Companion*. Two years earlier, Ford had asked Upham to take charge of the magazine's premium department. To encourage people to buy the magazine, the *Companion* offered free gifts, such as toys or books, with each subscription. These gifts were known as premiums. Readers could also buy products by mail. The premium department offered all kinds of goods—from silverware to jewelry to sewing machines.

The Youth's Companion gave away free gifts—called premiums—such as this calendar.

History of the American Flag

The United States adopted its first official flag on June 14, 1777. It had 13 white stars on a blue background and 13 red and white stripes to honor the 13 original American states. In 1795, after Vermont and Kentucky became states, two more stars and stripes were added. Government leaders realized, however, that as the country grew, adding a new stripe for each state would make the stripes too narrow or the flag too tall. To correct the problem, Congress redesigned the flag in 1818. Ever since, the American flag has had 13 stripes, but a star has been added for each new state. Today, the flag has 50 stars.

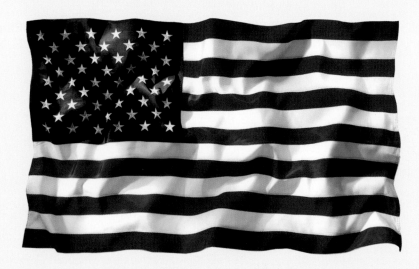

Upham decided to add American flags to the magazine's premium offerings. He put most of his energy into selling flags to schools. Students could write to the magazine to request 100 cards that they could then sell for a dime each. Each card said, "This Certificate entitles the holder thereof to one share in the patriotic influence of a Flag over the schoolhouse." After collecting 100 dimes, students would have the $10 needed to buy a flag from the *Companion*. Teachers and government leaders liked the idea. In 1891 alone, more than 25,000 schools purchased flags from the magazine.

Today, every public school is required by law to fly the American flag. These students in Goodsprings, Nevada, raise a flag at their school.

"Though there are still many schools which are not as yet provided with the flag, no public school shall be too poor, too remote or too indifferent to have the stars and stripes float over its roof."

—James Upham in
The Youth's Companion, 1890

Pleased with the success of his "Flag over the Schoolhouse" campaign, Upham started thinking about other ways to inspire patriotism. He knew that in October 1892, Americans would remember an important event. It would be the 400th anniversary of explorer Christopher Columbus's arrival in North America. Upham wanted all public schools to celebrate in the same way—with a **salute** to the American flag.

The Pledge

Upham wrote articles in *The Youth's Companion* asking readers if they liked his Columbus Day idea. The answer was "yes." Soon Upham's plan for saluting the flag became part of a bigger idea—a National Public School Celebration. This event would honor America's public schools. The idea soon gained the support of the National Education Association.

"We the youth of America, who today unite to march as one army under the sacred flag, understand our duty. We pledge ourselves that the flag shall not be stained; and that America shall mean equal opportunity and justice for every citizen and brotherhood for the world."

—From the speech "The Address for Columbus Day," part of the National Public School Celebration, written by Francis Bellamy, 1892

President Benjamin Harrison supported the idea of a National Public School Celebration.

For help in planning the event, Upham counted on Francis Bellamy. Bellamy had just been hired to work at the *Companion*. He was excited about the celebration. He wrote **press releases** about the event and sent them to newspapers in more than 4,000 cities and towns. Bellamy even helped convince President Benjamin Harrison to support the plans. On July 21, 1892, the president declared, "Let the National Flag float over every schoolhouse in the country, and…impress upon our youth the patriotic duties of American citizenship."

Francis Bellamy was born in Mount Morris, New York, in 1855. Like his father, Bellamy became a Baptist minister. He preached at a church in Boston, Massachusetts, and soon became known for his charity work among the poor. Bellamy believed in socialism. In a socialist country, the government owns all businesses. Bellamy saw that many Americans were very poor. He felt that if the U.S. government controlled businesses, it would make sure everyone had enough money to live a decent life. But many church members disagreed with his socialist beliefs and forced him to leave the church.

In 1891, Bellamy joined the staff of *The Youth's Companion*, where he wrote the Pledge of Allegiance. After leaving the *Companion* in 1896, Bellamy held jobs at several other magazines. He later was an account manager at a New York City advertising agency. Bellamy died in 1931 at the age of 76.

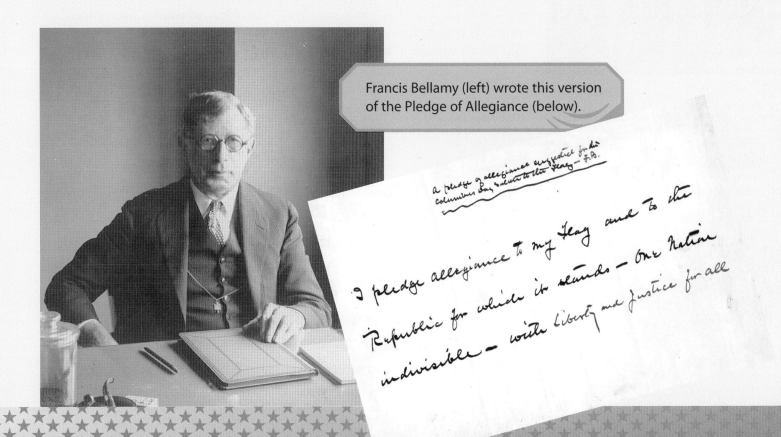

Francis Bellamy (left) wrote this version of the Pledge of Allegiance (below).

On Columbus Day 1892, the residents of New York City celebrated with a military parade.

This statue of explorer Christopher Columbus stands in Connecticut. Columbus Day celebrates his arrival in North America in 1492.

Working together, Upham and Bellamy wrote a program that every school could follow. Students would sing patriotic songs and make speeches. Raising the U.S. flag would be the highlight of the ceremony. Upham thought students should salute the flag and recite a pledge of loyalty to the United States. He wrote several versions of a pledge, but he wasn't happy with them. Upham thought Bellamy could do a better job. Bellamy's pledge was printed in the "Official Programme" for the "National Columbus Public School Celebration." This program was first published in *The Youth's Companion* on September 8, 1892.

On Columbus Day, more than 12 million students all over the country saluted as the American flag was raised above their schools. Together, they recited Bellamy's words: "I pledge allegiance to my Flag and to the Republic for which it stands—one nation, indivisible—with liberty and justice for all."

Along with the Pledge of Allegiance, Francis Bellamy created a salute to the flag. When saying the words "my Flag," students were told to extend their right arm toward the flag, with their palms facing up. The "Bellamy salute" was used until the United States began fighting Germany in World War II (1939–1945). Because Bellamy's salute was similar to one used by the German people and members of the ruling Nazi Party, Congress decided to invent a new salute. In 1942, the federal government first recognized the pledge as part of the U.S. Flag Code. This law now said that instead of extending the right arm, Americans were to place the right hand on the heart while saying the pledge. Americans still salute the flag in this way today.

Students and their teachers give the "Bellamy salute" as they say the Pledge of Allegiance.

The Pledge Changes

Francis Bellamy's pledge caught on quickly. It became a regular part of the day in many schools. By the early 1900s, children and adults alike recited it at public occasions. The pledge became especially popular after the United States entered World War I (1914–1918) in 1917. By the early 1920s, states started to pass laws requiring students to say the Pledge of Allegiance.

Over the years, the wording of the pledge changed. The first change came on June 14, 1923, during the National Flag Conference. The people attending the conference voted to change "my Flag" to "the Flag of the United States." They wanted recent **immigrants** to understand that they were saluting the American flag, not the flag of their homeland.

In schools across the United States, students started their day by saying the Pledge of Allegiance.

At the 1924 National Flag Conference, "of America" was added after "United States." This version of the pledge became part of the U.S. Flag Code on June 22, 1942. The Pledge of Allegiance was now part of a **federal** law. Only the government could make changes.

The pledge went through a final change in 1954. A Catholic group called the Knights of Columbus, supported by many other groups, convinced Congress to add "under God" after "one nation." At the time, the United States was close to war with the Soviet Union. The Soviet government didn't allow its people to worship freely. The Knights of Columbus thought the pledge should show that Americans, unlike the Soviets, had religious freedom.

Over the years, the pledge has been the subject of many national debates. The first dealt with who actually wrote it. In 1923, Bellamy claimed he was its author. Some people, however, thought it was actually written by Upham. In 1939, the U.S. Flag Association studied the matter. It found that Bellamy was the pledge's true author.

Members of the Knights of Columbus stand at attention during a church service. Men in the Knights of Columbus give support to families who belong to the Catholic Church. In 1954, the group asked Congress to add the words "under God" to the pledge.

"I learned the Pledge of Allegiance before the words under God were inserted into it. We did not know anything was missing…After 1954, whenever I heard the pledge recited, it sounded somehow tampered with and wrong. The original version had been grooved into my brain. I mistrusted the addition of under God…"

—Lance Morrow, *Time*, July 8, 2002

A more serious argument over the pledge arose in the early 1940s. By that time, most public school students were required to say the pledge daily. One group, however, objected to this practice. They were the Jehovah's Witnesses. Members of this religious faith believed pledging allegiance to anything but God was wrong.

In October 1935, 10-year-old Billy Gobitas and his 12-year-old sister, Lillian, refused to say the pledge in class. Both were expelled from their school in Minersville, Pennsylvania. Their parents, who were Jehovah's Witnesses, sued the school board. In 1940, the case was heard by the U.S. Supreme Court. The Supreme Court found that public schools did have the right to force children to say the pledge.

Billy and Lillian Gobitas, pictured here with their father, were expelled from school in 1935 for refusing to say the Pledge of Allegiance. Members of the Jehovah's Witnesses, the Gobitas children said reciting the pledge went against their religious beliefs.

Three years later, a group of Jehovah's Witnesses challenged this ruling. After hearing the case of *West Virginia State Board of Education* v. *Barnette*, the Supreme Court changed its mind. It found that forcing children to say the pledge was illegal. The justices said it went against the children's right to free speech. The Constitution says people in the United States can speak freely—or not speak—as they wish. It is now against the law to force any American to say the Pledge of Allegiance.

Saying the Pledge

The respectful way to say the Pledge of Allegiance is to face the flag, stand straight, and place your right hand over your heart. If a man is wearing a hat and he is not in uniform, he should remove the hat with his right hand and hold it at his left shoulder. People in uniform are asked to remain silent while the pledge is spoken. They should face the flag and give it a military salute.

When the Pledge of Allegiance is recited, people in uniform should salute. People not in uniform should place their right hand over their heart.

The Pledge's Meaning

President George W. Bush (lower left) delivers the State of the Union address before Congress. The word "republic" in the Pledge of Allegiance reminds Americans that they are responsible for electing leaders to govern the nation.

Francis Bellamy chose the words for the Pledge of Allegiance carefully. He knew that each word would need to have great meaning. The pledge begins with "I pledge allegiance." A pledge is a promise. Allegiance means loyalty. With these words, we are promising to be true "to the Flag of the United States of America."

We also say we will be loyal "to the Republic for which it stands." With the word "republic," Bellamy reminds us of America's form of government. In some countries, kings, queens, or **dictators** rule the people. In a republic, the citizens rule by choosing representatives to govern their country. In the United States, this means we elect leaders such as the president and members of Congress to make our laws.

The words "for which it stands" mean that the flag is a **symbol** for the United States and its government. When we pledge our loyalty to the flag, we are also promising to be loyal to the country it stands for.

The pledge continues with a description of America. It says the United States is "one nation." All 50 states and the territories have joined together to make one country. It also means that even though Americans come from many backgrounds, we will all stand together.

The words "under God" were added to show the importance of religious faith in the lives of many Americans. When the phrase was inserted, President Dwight D. Eisenhower called this faith "our country's most powerful resource in peace and war."

The words "one nation" in the pledge mean that Americans will stand together to support their country.

During the Civil War, when the North battled the South, the United States was a nation divided. Written after this war, the Pledge of Allegiance says the country is now "indivisible."

The United States is also "indivisible." To Francis Bellamy, these were possibly the most important words of the pledge. When he wrote them, the Civil War was fresh in the minds of many Americans. During this conflict, states in the South tried to break away from the rest of the nation and create their own country. States in the North went to war with the South to stop them. The North won the war, and the United States remained one nation. By calling the nation "indivisible," Bellamy was saying the country would never be divided into separate pieces. Despite the problems of the past, America will always stay strong and united.

To end the pledge, Bellamy considered including the words "liberty, **equality**, **fraternity**"—a phrase that was used during the French Revolution in the 1700s. But Bellamy was troubled by the word "equality." He realized that not all Americans were being treated the same. In 1892, women, blacks, and people of other backgrounds often did not have the same rights as white males. He also chose not to use "fraternity," which means a sense of community and friendship. Bellamy felt no people had yet achieved true fraternity. He once wrote that the idea that the United States offered real equality and fraternity was "too fanciful, too many thousands of years off in realization."

Throughout the 1800s and early 1900s, women fought for the right to vote. They won this right in 1920, when the 19th Amendment to the Constitution became law.

Blacks fought for equal rights well into the 1900s. In 1963, more than 250,000 people marched to the Lincoln Memorial in Washington, D.C. They protested for equal treatment under the law for blacks and all other Americans.

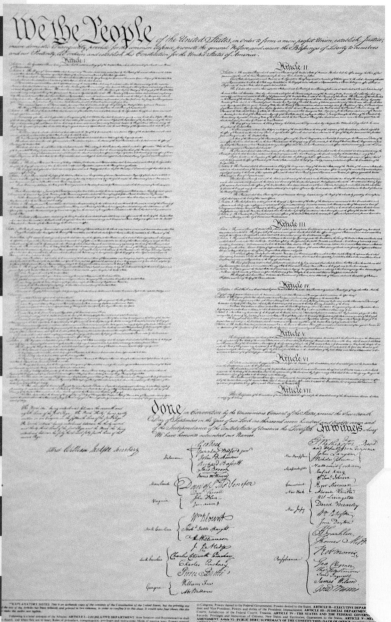

Yet Bellamy was confident that "we as a nation do stand square on the doctrine of liberty and justice for all." Liberty means freedom. All Americans are free to make their own choices. Justice is fairness. By law, Americans have the right to be treated fairly. To many Americans, it is these last six words, "with liberty and justice for all," that celebrate the true spirit of the United States.

The final words of the Pledge of Allegiance speak of liberty and justice. One of the goals of the Constitution, which is the basis of the U.S. government, is to ensure justice and liberty for all Americans.

I pledge allegiance to the Flag
of the United States of America,
and to the Republic for which it stands,
one Nation under God, indivisible,
with liberty and justice for all.

What Do the Words Mean?

allegiance: loyalty

indivisible: unable to be divided

justice: fairness

liberty: freedom

nation: country

pledge: to promise

republic: any government that is not ruled by
a king or queen; the United States is a
republic in which citizens elect the leaders.

The American flag is a symbol of the United
States. When we pledge allegiance to the flag,
we are promising to be loyal to our country.

The Pledge Today

Since schoolchildren first recited it in 1892, the Pledge of Allegiance has become part of the daily life of millions of Americans. It is most often heard in public and private schools. More than three-fourths of all states have passed laws that encourage students to say the pledge every day or at least once a week.

Many organizations also ask their members to say the pledge during meetings. Among them are the Boy Scouts, Girl Scouts, 4-H Club, Elks Club, and American Legion. Many government leaders regularly pledge allegiance to the flag. They include the members of Congress, as well as many state lawmakers and members of city and county councils.

Over the years, however, some people have questioned the worth of the pledge. They believe many Americans say the words thoughtlessly, without stopping to consider what they mean. The words "under God" in the pledge also bother many people. They believe it's not right to include religion in a promise of loyalty to America. When the country was founded, the idea of keeping religion and the government separate was very important to people. That division, some say, should always be clear.

The Boy Scouts is one of many groups that say the Pledge of Allegiance at their meetings.

The U.S. Flag Code includes all national laws about how the American flag should be used and displayed. The Pledge of Allegiance and how it is said are part of this flag code. Here are some of the code's other rules:

★ The flag should be raised quickly and lowered slowly and solemnly.

★ The flag should be flown only from sunrise to sunset unless a light is shined on it at night. It should not be flown during bad weather unless it is an all-weather flag.

★ Americans should raise the flag every day, but especially on holidays.

★ The flag should be displayed every day in front of public buildings, including schools. On Election Day, voting places should also display the flag.

★ The president can order the flag to be flown at "half-staff"—the halfway point on a flagpole—to honor government leaders or other people who have died.

To see all the rules in the U.S. Flag Code, visit this Internet site:

www4.law.cornell.edu/uscode/4/ch1.html

The U.S. flag flies over government buildings, including the White House in Washington, D.C. When this photograph was taken, the flag was flying at half-staff.

The U.S. Flag Code encourages Americans to fly the flag every day.

For many Americans, the meaning of the Pledge of Allegiance deepens during troubled times. On September 11, 2001, terrorists attacked America. They took control of airplanes and flew them into the World Trade Center in New York City and the Pentagon in Washington, D.C. Another plane crashed into a field in Pennsylvania. Altogether, the terrorists killed nearly 3,000 people. When the United States celebrated Columbus Day the next month, children across the country all stood to say the Pledge of Allegiance at the same time. Together, they promised their loyalty to their country, reminding the world the United States would endure. This sight gave many Americans hope and strength.

The Pledge of Allegiance remains a treasured part of American life. Despite the complaints it has drawn, Americans continue to teach the pledge to their children. And by saying its words, they are reminded of the great goals of their country—to ensure "liberty and justice for all."

Fire fighters and soldiers hang a flag at the Pentagon in Washington, D.C., to honor the people killed by terrorists on September 11, 2001.

"In the moments after September 11, Americans turned instinctively to the flag we share...No authority of government can ever prevent an American from pledging allegiance to this one nation under God."
—President George W. Bush, July 4, 2002

★ Many historians say a statesman named Francis Hopkinson had the idea for the American flag's stars and stripes design. But no one knows for sure who made the first flag. Legend says that in 1776, George Washington hired a Philadelphia seamstress named Betsy Ross to sew the design.

★ The stars and stripes design was approved as the official U.S. flag on June 14, 1777. We celebrate Flag Day every year on June 14.

★ When the government approved the flag's design, it did not say what the colors meant. The government did, however, give the colors meaning when they were chosen for the Great Seal of the United States. On the seal, red stands for strength and bravery, white stands for purity and innocence, and blue stands for loyalty and justice.

★ The U.S. flag goes by many nicknames, including Old Glory; The Stars and Stripes; The Star-Spangled Banner; and The Red, White, and Blue.

★ The American flag has flown in some faraway places. In 1909, American Robert Peary became the first person to reach the North Pole. He placed a U.S. flag there. In 1963, mountain climber Barry Bishop planted the American flag on Mount Everest in Asia, the highest mountain in the world. And in 1969, astronaut Neil Armstrong flew the American flag on the Moon.

An astronaut salutes the American flag on the Moon.

August 1892

Francis Bellamy writes the Pledge of Allegiance.

September 8, 1892

The pledge is published in *The Youth's Companion.*

October 21, 1892

More than 12 million schoolchildren recite the pledge as part of National Public Schools Celebration of Columbus Day.

June 14, 1923

The words "my Flag" in the pledge are changed to "the Flag of the United States" at the National Flag Conference.

1888

The Youth's Companion begins a campaign to sell American flags to its readership.

June 14, 1777

The United States adopts the stars and stripes design as the official flag.

June 14, 1924

The words "of America" are added after "the Flag of the United States" during the National Flag Conference.

1920

1890

1880

1780

June 3, 1940

The Supreme Court rules against Lillian and Billy Gobitas; public school students, it said, can be forced to recite the pledge.

June 22, 1942

The pledge becomes part of the U.S. Flag Code.

June 14, 1943

In the case of *West Virginia State Board of Education v. Barnette*, the Supreme Court reverses its 1940 decision; no one can be forced to recite the pledge.

June 26, 2002

The Ninth Circuit Court of Appeals declares that saying the pledge in public schools is unconstitutional.

June 14, 1954

President Dwight D. Eisenhower signs a law adding the words "under God" to the pledge.

1930   1940   1950   2000

America in 1892

Students across the country said the Pledge of Allegiance for the first time in 1892. What else was happening in the United States that year?

★ The United States is made up of 44 states.

★ The president is Benjamin Harrison.

★ The immigration station opens at Ellis Island in New York.

★ Susan B. Anthony becomes the president of the National American Woman Suffrage Association. This group works to gain voting rights for women.

★ In Wyoming, wealthy cattlemen battle small ranchers in the Johnson County War.

★ Workers in Idaho's lead and silver mines go on strike.

★ The clothes dryer, the electric radiator, the gasoline-powered automobile, and the matchbook are invented.

★ The government opens 3 million acres (1.2 million hectares) of land owned by the Cheyenne and Arapaho Indians to settlement by non-Indians.

Constitution (kon-stuh-TOO-shun) the written document that is the basis for the U.S. government

dictator (DIK-tay-tuhr) a leader who has complete control over a country

equality (ee-KWAL-uh-tee) when everyone has the same rights

federal (FED-uh-ruhl) in a federal government, individual parts of a country—such as states—are joined under one central government; the federal government is this central government.

fraternity (fruh-TER-nah-tee) a feeling of community and friendship

immigrant (IM-uh-gruhnt) someone who leaves one country and settles in another country

lawsuit (LAW-soot) action taken against a person or a group in a court of law

patriotism (PAY-tree-uh-tiz-uhm) the love a person has for his or her country

press release (PRES ruh-LEES) a written announcement sent out to newspapers and organizations

salute (suh-LOOT) to raise your hand as a sign of honor and respect

symbol (SIM-buhl) something that stands for something else; the American flag is a symbol for the United States.

un-American (UN-uh-MAYR-uh-kuhn) against the best interests of the American people

Newly sworn-in American citizens say the Pledge of Allegiance during a ceremony in San Jose, California.

To Learn More

READ THESE BOOKS

Herbert, Janis. *The Civil War Book for Kids: A History with 21 Activities*. Chicago: Chicago Review Press, 1999.

Quiri, Patricia Ryon. *The American Flag*. New York: Children's Press, 1998.

Raatma, Lucia. *Patriotism*. Mankato, Minn.: Bridgestone Books, 2000.

Swanson, June. *I Pledge Allegiance*. Minneapolis: Carolrhoda Books, 2002.

Webster, Christine. *The Pledge of Allegiance*. New York: Children's Press, 2003.

LOOK UP THESE INTERNET SITES

The American Legion
www.legion.org/our_flag/of_main.htm
The "Our Flag" section of the American Legion's web site offers information about displaying the American flag and saying the pledge.

The Flag of the United States of America and the Pledge of Allegiance
www.usflag.org
The "Table of Contents" section of this web site links to information about the history of the U.S. flag, rules for flying the flag, and patriotic writings.

Nineteenth Century American Children and What They Read
www.merrycoz.org/MAGS2.HTM#yc
This site collects articles from a number of 19th-century magazines, including *The Youth's Companion*.

Pledge Questions and Answers
www.pledgeqanda.com
This site gives answers to commonly asked questions about the Pledge of Allegiance.

The Star-Spangled Banner Flag House
www.flaghouse.org/about/a_flag.html
The museum site discusses the history of the Pledge of Allegiance, the American flag, and "The Star-Spangled Banner," the national anthem of the United States.

INTERNET SEARCH KEY WORDS:

Pledge of Allegiance, Francis Bellamy, The Youth's Companion, Columbus Day, U.S. flag, Flag Day

Index